LET'S FACE IT!

LET'S FACE IT!
Kai Heinonen's World

PHAEDRA INC.—Publishers   49 Park Avenue, New York, N.Y. 10016

Phaedra Inc.—Publishers

Copyright © 1971 by Kai Heinonen

Library of Congress Card Number 70-156218

All Rights Reserved. No part of this book may be reproduced in any form without the permission of the Publisher, Phaedra Inc., 49 Park Avenue, New York, N.Y. 10016

First Edition

September 1971

Manufactured in the United States of America

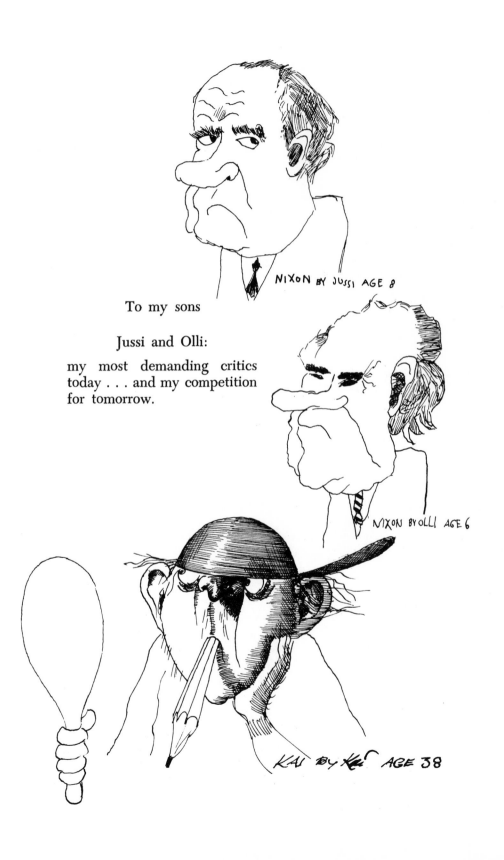

NIXON BY JUSSI AGE 8

To my sons

Jussi and Olli:

my most demanding critics
today . . . and my competition
for tomorrow.

NIXON BY OLLI AGE 6

KAL BY KAL AGE 38

INDEX

LET'S FACE IT!

NIXON: "What we would like to do is to extricate ourselves
without exactly leaving."

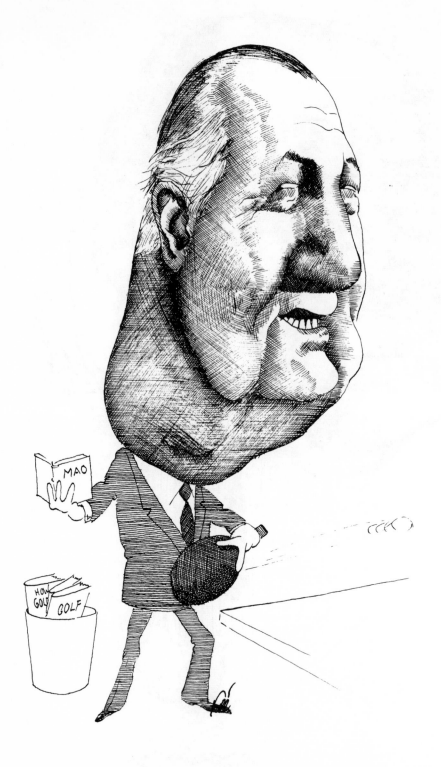

AGNEW: "Any rumors that Richard Nixon will not be on the ticket with me in 1972 are totally without foundation."

JOHN MITCHELL: "This country's going so far right, you're not even going to recognize it."

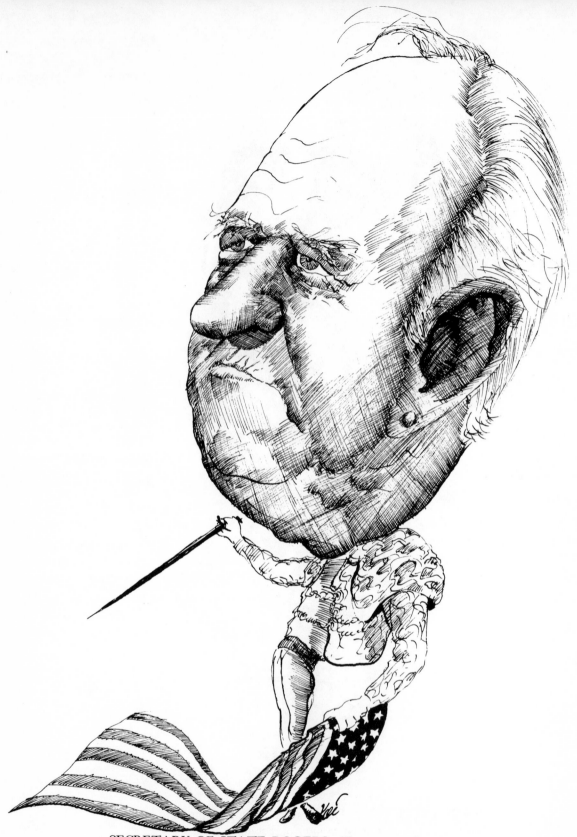

SECRETARY OF STATE ROGERS: "I want to show a new
interest in Africa, Asia . . . Europe . . ."

MELVIN LAIRD: "Our policy is based on preventive war, not planning to fight wars." "The intelligence on this mission was excellent of course, the Son Tay raid wasn't a disaster . . . it's just that."

5

JOHN CONNALLY: "Smooth politico."

JUSTICE BURGER: "Warrenburger after earlwarren."

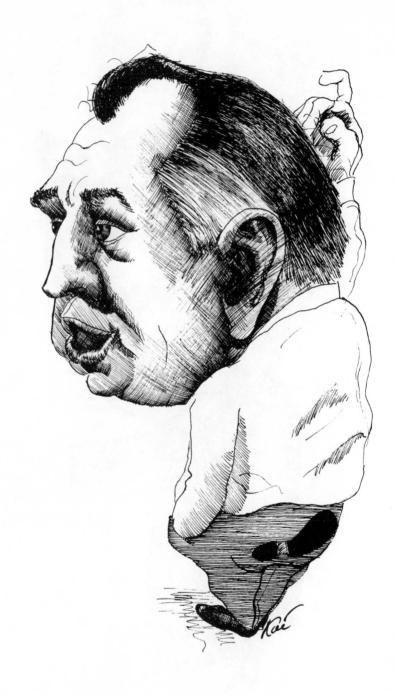

WALTER J. HICKEL: ("Out with a bang, not a whimper.")
"I suppose I've done everything to deserve being fired."

RAMSEY CLARK: "Like a jellyfish."—J. E. Hoover.

BEBE REBOZO: "Nixon likes to be alone, and with Bebe along, he is."

HARRY TRUMAN: "a statesman is a politician who's been
dead ten or 15 years."

LYNDON JOHNSON: "In these days, the fate of this office
is the fate of us all."

LADY BIRD JOHNSON: "You never can tell whom you'll
meet in Lyndon's bedroom . . . I walked in and who should
be sitting there but . . . Richard Nixon!"

13

DEAN RUSK: "The problem of Vietnam has a tendency to close doors."

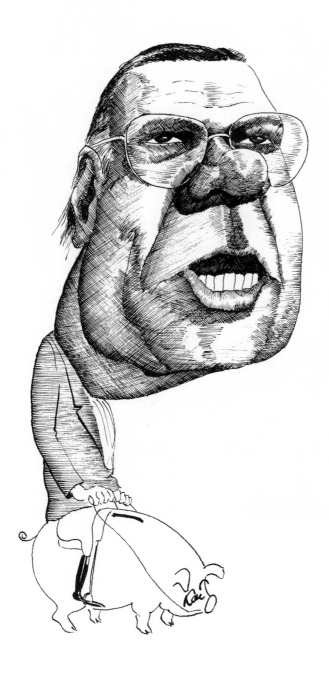

ROBERT McNAMARA: "Not to quantify what can be qualified
is to be content with less than the full range of reason."

J. EDGAR HOOVER: "Extenuating circumstances." (National Guard fire at Kent State.)

PATRICK MURPHY: "If this is freedom in its finest form, it
is also freedom in its final hour."

KISSINGER: "The playboy of the Western Wing."

HUGH HEFNER: "I would rather meet a girl and fall in love and have her fall in love with me than make another 100 million dollars."

GOLDA MEIR: "Nixon gives us sweet words and Rogers stabs us in the back."

ABBA EBAN: "Quite demonstrably, we are not shaking in
our boots."

MOSHE DAYAN: "You know, people have very big appetites, and that includes us in Israel too."

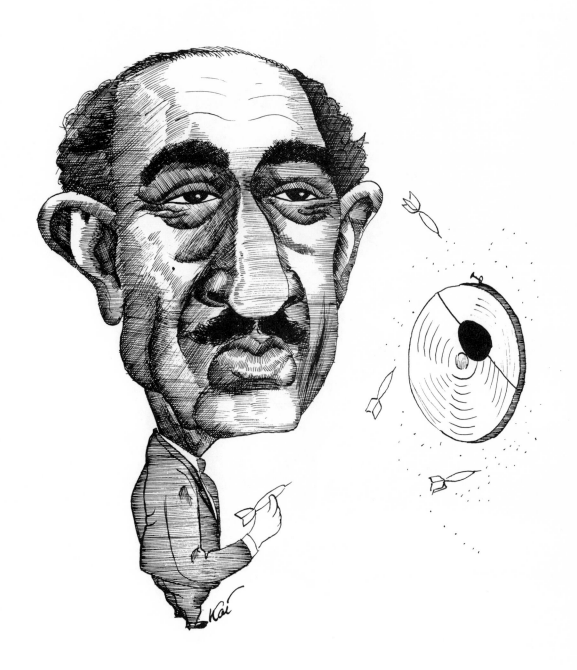

ANWAR SADAT: "There will be no compromise . . . and we will not give up an inch of our land."

NASSER: "In the Arab world there is a role wandering aimlessly
in search of a hero."

HUSSEIN: "I'm not the sort of person who can quit."

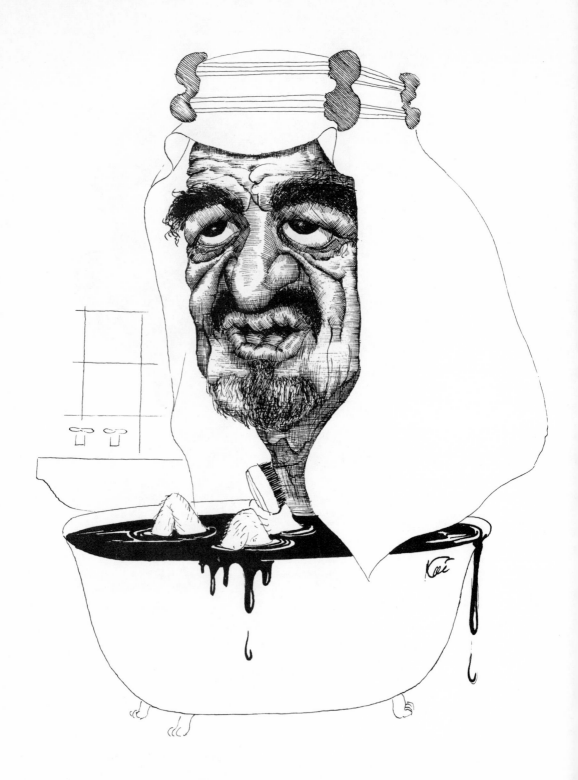

KING FAISAL: "Communism is a Zionist creation designed to fulfill the aims of Zionism."

GUNNAR JARRING: "An impeccably behaved Western Union messenger."

U THANT: "I speak not as the Secretary-General of the United Nations, not as an Asian, not as a Burmese, but as a human being, a member of that species, Homo sapiens, whose continued existence is in the balance."

MAO: "Revolution is not a dinner party, nor an essay, nor a painting, nor a piece of embroidery; it cannot be advanced softly, gradually, carefully, considerately, respectfully, politely, plainly and modestly."

LEONID BREZHNEV: "Party Boss Leonid Brezhnev held the
rostrum, and was interrupted by dutiful applause no fewer than
169 times."—24th Communist Party Congress.
"You know, comrades," said Brezhnev, "none of us is entrusted
with positions of authority in perpetuity."

KOSYGIN: "No one can doubt the peaceful policy of the
Soviet Union, and we shall pursue it firmly and consistently."

PRES. THIEU: "I never neutralize."

GEN. WESTMORELAND: "The revolution I envisage comes not from the helicopter alone." (He took 12 years to get pilot's license.)

NIKITA KHRUSHCHEV: "My time has come and gone. There's nothing I can do now but share my experiences with anyone who cares to listen."

FIDEL CASTRO: "History will absolve me." (La historia me
absolverá)

DR. S. ALLENDE: (No congratulations message from the
White House.) " . . . because it would be unseemly to con-
gratulate a Marxist victor in the Western hemisphere."

MARSHAL TITO: "One might be under the impression that somebody wanted to get rid of me."

DE GAULLE: "Politics are too serious a matter to be left
to politicians."

GEORGES POMPIDOU: "What I do after 9 p.m. is my own business."

WILLY BRANDT: "The times do not work automatically in
favor of reason and peace."

ARTE JOHNSON: "I ask the fellas to give me their old jackets
and I use them for overcoats."

WALTER ULBRICHT: "He has been in power longer than Hitler and almost as long as Bismarck."

FRANCISCO FRANCO: "The Caudillo is getting old."

SVEN OLOF PALME: "As Minister of Communications, Olof Palme helped steer the country from left- to right-hand traffic in 1967. According to his critics, that was the only time Olof has moved away from the left since he started shaving."

URHO KEKKONEN: "Neutrality with a Tilt."

45

INDIRA GANDHI: "Could a man do better?"

BERNADETTE DEVLIN: "A female Castro in a miniskirt."
"We were born into an unjust system; we are not prepared to
grow old in it."

"I am no saint, and not even an interesting sinner."

TRUDEAU: "Separatism a revolution? My eye."

EDWARD HEATH: "Will Heath's shock therapy cure the patient or send him into coma?"

PRINCE PHILIP: "I'm one of those stupid bums who never went to the university . . . and a fat lot of harm it did me."

PRINCE CHARLES: "George 3rd realized that England had more to gain when the American colonies were in rebellion, and that more advantages were to be reaped from their trade as friends rather than as colonies . . . he was right."

PRINCESS ANN: "I don't give interviews."

BELLA ABZUG: "This woman's place is in the house . . . of Representatives."

HUBERT HUMPHREY: "The right to be heard does not auto-matically include the right to be taken seriously."

SEN. MUSKIE: "I'll never say anything that won't improve on silence."

55

SEN. McGOVERN: "It's no secret that I'm very much in-
terested . . ." (pres. election)

EUGENE McCARTHY (& buttons): "If nothing else, they'll be worth something on the antiques market."

TEDDY KENNEDY: "I may not be Bobbie Orr, but I think my name is still a household word in Massachusetts."

ROSE KENNEDY: "I'm like old wine, when there is a special occasion in our family, they bring me out."

SEN. W. FULBRIGHT: "Waspish as always." "It is certainly a very provocative act to mount a physical invasion. It may lead to other things, who knows . . ."

SEN. MIKE MANSFIELD: "Things are just about in status
quo in all . . ."

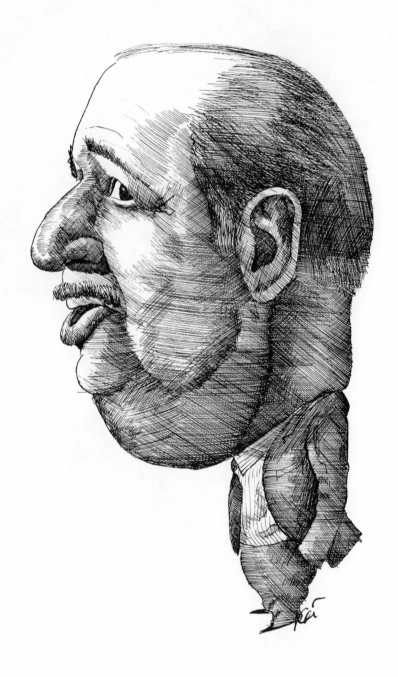

HUGH SCOTT: He says he is "the only barrier on the Republican side of the aisle to the southern strategy."

JIM BUCKLEY: "3 cheers for fear and hatred, division and mistrust, when Jim goes to Washington these will be a must."
—His supporters.

WILLIAM F. BUCKLEY: "The free market is an antidote to governmental manipulation in a world dominated by bureaucrats and the miiltary." (Since when has that disturbed Buckley?) "Stop calling me a crypto-Nazi or I'll sock you in your goddam face and you'll stay plastered." (To Gore Vidal)

NORMAN MAILER: "My notion of the law is that it was conceived to catch every whore and make every mean man rich."

JAMES RESTON: "This is a devilish thing about foreign affairs, they are foreign, and will not always conform to our whims."

WALTER LIPPMANN: Words

JIMMY BRESLIN: "My high school class produced 16 NYC policemen, 17 NYC firemen, and 32 of the most prominent felons in the city."

ART BUCHWALD: "I'm sympathetic to women's lib. I know from personal experience what it's like to be treated as a sex object."

HELEN GURLEY BROWN: "I think marriage is insurance for the worst years of life. During the best years you don't need a husband."

GLORIA STEINEM: "Let's not run scared unless we have to."

KATE MILLETT: " . . . dissection of sexual phallacy."

DR. SPOCK and his spooks: "The Pied Piper called in to get the habits out of rats by turning the kids into cats."—M. McLuhan.

WILLIAM KUNSTLER: "He's the blackest white man I ever saw."—George Fleming

JERRY RUBIN: "Our message is, don't grow up."

JUDGE J. HOFFMAN: "The Chicago 8 defense managed to
win one motion from him: early break for lunch" . . . "It is clear
that there is a circus in the courtroom, and that the judge is
the ringleader."—TV reporter.

ABBIE HOFFMAN: "My name is Abbie. I'm an orphan of Amerika."

GOV. WALLACE: "As your governor, I promise I won't do anything to embarrass you."

BOBBY SEALE: "Those were the days, man, dangerous days, laying around in jail and thinking about 1984."

LESTER MADDOX: "I hope to become the first ex-governor
to sell a million records."

ELDRIDGE CLEAVER: " . . . too much on ice in Algeria
to write."

MAYOR DALEY: "D for diligent, A for adorable, L for loyal,
E for energetic, Y for youthful."—His supporters.

ANGELA DAVIS: "We love you from the West Coast to the East Coast, and you *Will* be free."

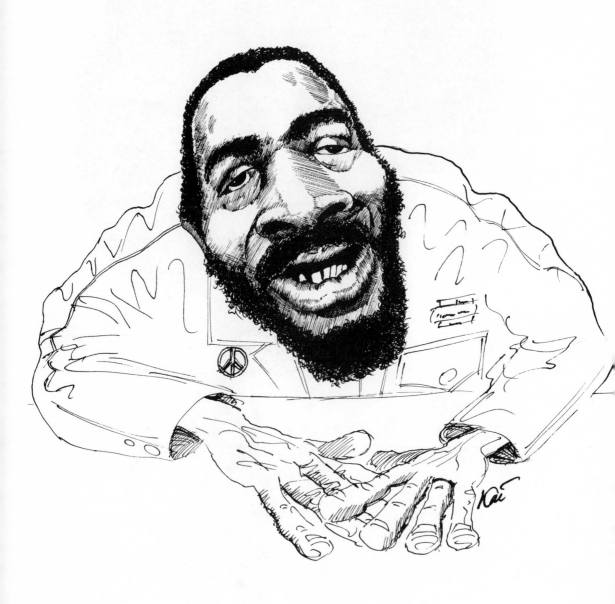

DICK GREGORY: "I waited around till the lunch counter integrated, and then they didn't have what I wanted."

MALCOLM X: "for every shut eye ain't asleep" . . . "and every
good-bye ain't gone"—Lewis Michaux.

GOV. REAGAN: "There is nothing the people of California
cannot do."

NELSON ROCKEFELLER: "Rock of Ages."

JOHN LINDSAY: "I suppose I'd be the best Scrooge in town."
(Reading Dickens' "Christmas Carol.")

ARTHUR GOLDBERG: "Yesterday I spent a week with Arthur
Goldberg."—A reporter.

W. SCRANTON: "A nation driven to use weapons of war upon its youth is a nation on the edge of chaos."

DANIEL P. MOYNIHAN: "There is no neglect like 'benign neglect.'"

THOMAS HOVING: "There will be a lot of screaming and yelling & nostalgia & recrimination." (Metropolitan Museum.)

MAYOR K. GIBSON: "I'm sure you never realized that someday
Newark would have soul."

DR. TIMOTHY LEARY: "Turn on, tune in, drop out."

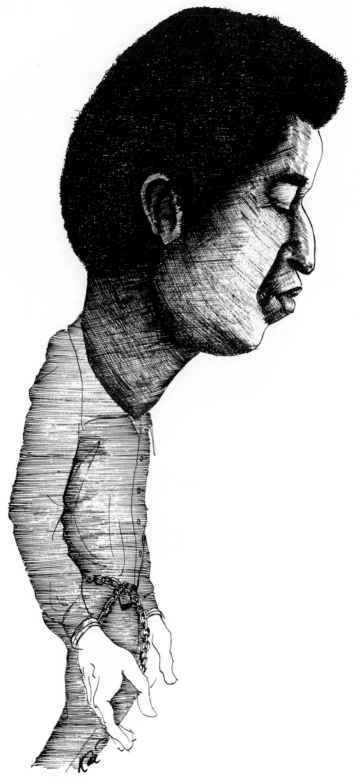

GEORGE JACKSON: "This is one nigger that's positively displeased. I'll never forgive, never forget . . . War without terms." (Soledad)

CÉSAR CHÁVEZ: "It's just great when people participate."
(in support, Harvard has banned non-union lettuce . . . can
any university do less?)

KINGMAN BREWSTER: "Many students have learned that Weathermen beget Minutemen and the rhetoric of Abbie and Jerry begets the counter-rhetoric of John and Martha." (Yale)

FATHERS DAN & PHILIP BERRIGAN: "Without us, you
could not talk as freely against the war as you do."

BILLY GRAHAM: "You can also get high on Jesus."

CARD. CUSHING: " . . . had a good word for everyone who
came down the pike . . . Billy Graham, NAACP, the John
Birch Society."

POPE PAUL: "In Italy they say that he's killed one bird with
2 stones." (The Pill.) "Pilgrim Pope."

DR. REUBEN: "After all, sex is just something people do."

E. SEGAL: "I can give you a list of all the guys at the New York Times who cried over my book." (*Love Story*.)

JACKIE ONASSIS: "All that counts now is money. It's people with money who are the real royalty these days."

MARIA CALLAS: " . . . she's not overindulgent or overforgiving
or too generous for her own good, or anything like that."

JACQUELINE SUSANN: "I don't think words in themselves
are dirty."

PHILIP ROTH: "Every month I get a letter from the government saying 'Congratulations, you've just sponsored another B-52 raid on Vietnam.'"

TRUMAN CAPOTE: "I don't care what anybody says about me as long as it isn't true."

ALLEN GINSBERG: "Exactly the same exactly the same exactly the same with no purpose but grimness."

KURT VONNEGUT: "I used to be a PR man for General Electric, then I became a free lance writer of so-called slick fiction . . . both bugger truth for money."

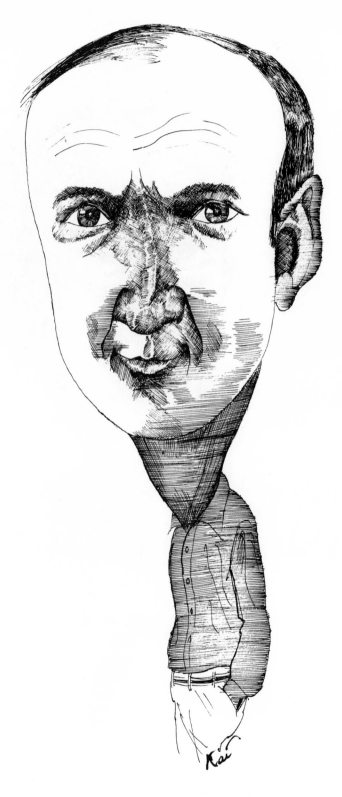

NEIL SIMON: "How funny and sad life is."

KENNETH TYNAN: "A critic is a man who knows the way, but can't drive a car."

SUSAN SONTAG: "Once upon a time it must have been a revolutionary and creative move to interpret works of art."

JAMES JONES: "If the world were to be blow up I mean
that I could even enjoy the spectacle—though I wouldn't be able
to write about it."

JAMES BALDWIN: "For me, writing was an act of love. . . . It was an attempt to be loved."

SAUL BELLOW: "I count . . . Not on perfect understanding, which is Cartesian, but on approximate understanding, which is Jewish. And on a meeting of sympathies, which is human."

TOM WOLFE: " 'Radical chic' slumming and integrating in the
fashionable new politics."

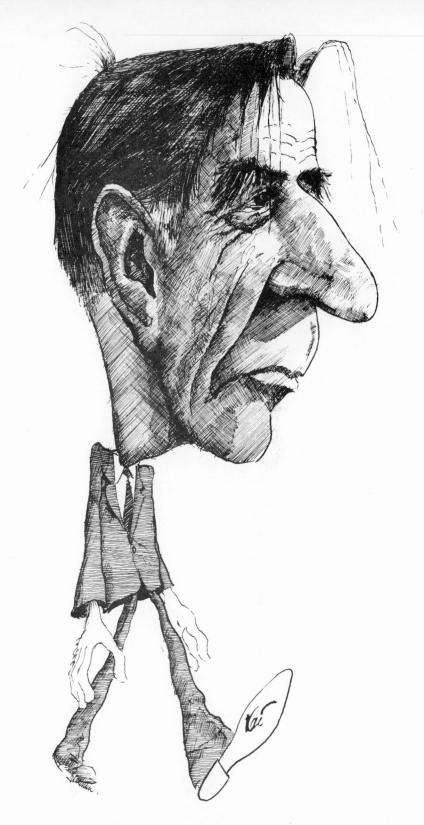

GALBRAITH: "The American ambassador is an anachronism."

SAMUEL BECKETT: "Words have been my only love." (More pricks than kicks.) "A frightful experience, New York. Never again!"

ERNEST HEMINGWAY: Papa

WILLIAM SAROYAN: "Either I myself was the beginning and end of the matter, or there was no matter at all."

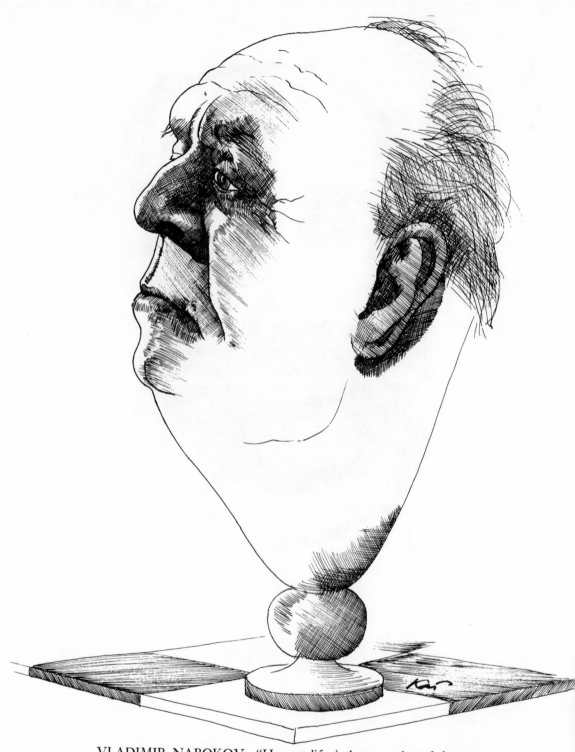

VLADIMIR NABOKOV: "Human life is but a series of foot-
notes to a vast obscure unfinished masterpiece."
"A syllogism: other men die; but I am not another; therefore
I'll not die."

SOLZHENITSYN: "A great writer is like a second government.
That's why no regime anywhere, has ever loved its great writers,
only it minor ones."

MARSHALL McLUHAN: "Hello, is that M.M.? at the White House we're having a little difficulty in communicating with North Vietnam, Russia, America . . . Is it our medium or our message?"

CASEY STENGEL: "The Mets are a team that has come along slow but fast."

MARIO PUZO: "At first I thought it was trash. Now I think its pretty good. If I'd taken it seriously when I sat down to write, it might have been great."

FRANK SINATRA: "Unwanted as a child, now he's wanted in five states."

DEAN MARTIN: "Make-a-million Martin."

SAMMY DAVIS Jr.: "Talk about handicap—I'm a one-eyed
Negro Jew."

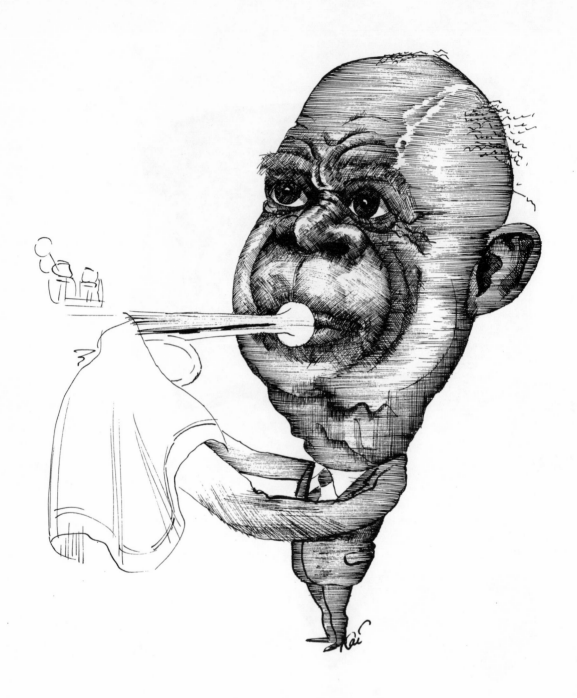

LOUIS ARMSTRONG: " . . . people don't like for me to talk
about the olden days. All the prosty-toots and the fine gage and
the bad-ass racketeers. But hell, Man, I got to tell it like it was.
I can't go around changing history."

JOHNNIE CASH: "I walk the line."

BARBRA STREISAND: "I believe in rhythm."

TINY TIM: "Since coming into the world as Herbert Khaury, he has been known by various aliases, among them, Emmett Swink, Rolli Dell, Darry Dover, and Larry Love, the Singing Canary."

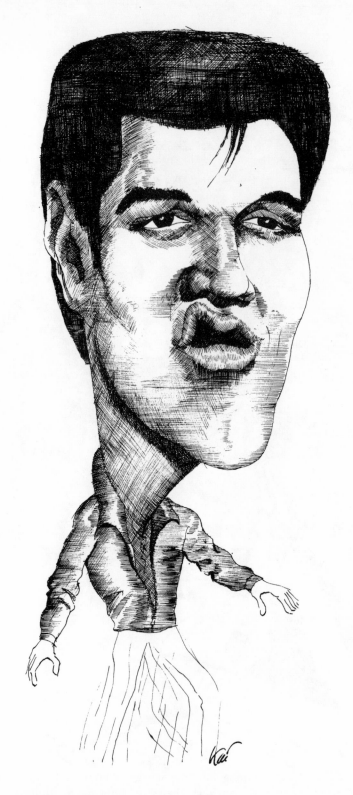

ELVIS PRESLEY: "Shaking, gyrating and quivering . . ."

THE BEATLES: "Let It Be" . . . "The End"
Would you like an "Apple"?
"Nothing in life really stays. And its beautiful that they go. They
have to go in order for the next thing to come." Paul McCartney.

SIMON & GARFUNKEL: "How terribly strange to be in '70."

JOAN BAEZ: "Hush, little boy, don't you cry, your momma's gone now for to march."

BOB DYLAN: "The underground's outta work sing the bells of New York—The underground's more dangerous ring the bells of Los Angeles."

138

JAMES TAYLOR: "With all that feedback of ideas and memories and resonances from the past, an interview can be like an epileptic fit." . . . "Sweet Baby James."

JANIS JOPLIN: (Pearl) "look at me, man, I'm selling my heart."

JIMI HENDRIX: "I'm not going to have a funeral . . . I'm
going to have a jam-session."

GLEN CAMPBELL: "My approach is simplicity. If I can make
a forty-year-old housewife put down her dishtowel and say 'Oh'—
why then, man, I've got it made."

BURT BACHARACH: "Everybody's composer."

LEONARD BERNSTEIN: "Enough with black-white-red-
pinko-Commie-fascist-faggot-hippiehatreds."

144

ARTUR RUBINSTEIN: "When they praise me, it bores me, when they pan me, it annoys me."

AARON COPLAND: "Composers tend to assume that everyone
loves music. Surprisingly enough, everyone doesn't."

IGOR STRAVINSKY: "I am a composer myself, and I must cultivate my own garden."

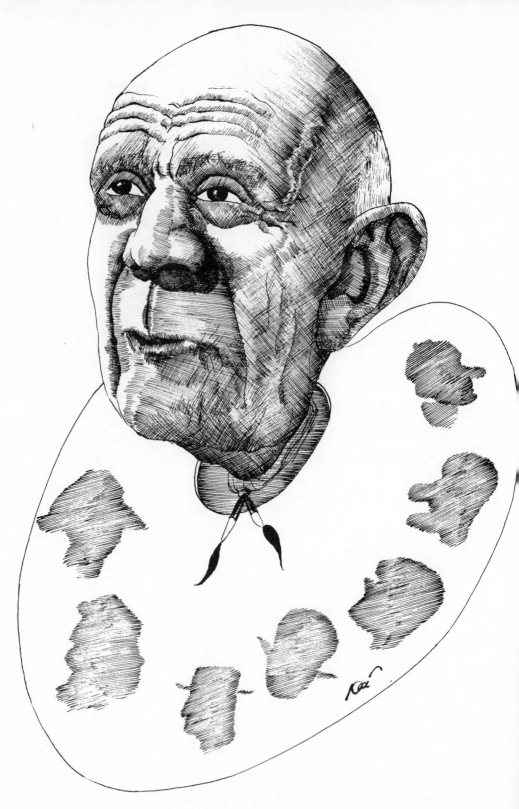

PICASSO: "To draw you must close your eyes and sing."

SALVADOR DALI: "This is the divine Dali speaking . . . I do
not take drugs, I *am* drugs."

ANDY WARHOL: "Following in the trash, gay gland tradition . . ." (About his movie, "Trash.")

AL CAPP (re. J. Buckley): "It used to be that you only admitted to being a conservative to your rabbi, priest or family doctor. Now, it appears it is legal to practice conservatism between consenting adults."

BUCKMINSTER FULLER: "God is a verb the most active connoting the vast harmonic . . . from unleashed chaos of energy."

NEIL ARMSTRONG: "The difference between eternity and life is about one hundredth of an inch of rubber."

DR. BARNARD: "Are heart transplants really justified?"
"yes," said Barnard . . . He has performed five such operations,
and his patients have survived a total of 1,101 days—or an average
of 220 days. Other heart patients who were accepted for transplants in Cape Town and Stanford, but who died because no
donor became available, survived an average of only 30 days.
"So," said Barnard, "we have an improvement of about 600%."

ERIK ERIKSON: "If ever an identity crisis was central and long-drawn out in somebody's life, it was so in mine."

DR. LINUS PAULING: "Peace and Vitamin C."

156

MARGARET MEAD: "We women play for real . . . to win."

RALPH NADER: "If you really believe that cars are unsafe, meat and fish unhealthy, TV gives off harmful rays, jets are dangerous and the air is polluted, you are apt to live a little like a nun."

HENRY FORD II: "We're making an intensified effort to minimize pollution."

DAVID ROCKEFELLER: "Not Olive Oil."

LORD ROY THOMSON: "Each morning, when Lord Thomson of Fleet wakes up in Buckinghamshire, he can never be quite sure how many newspapers he owns."

ROBERT HAACK: "There were times when I slept very well
between 2.15 a.m. and 2.30 a.m."

HOWARD HUGHES: "I suppose I am not like other men . . ."
("At times he was seen wearing empty kleenex boxes on his feet,
apparently to guard against germs . . .")
Invisible Man

BOB HOPE: "Thank you very much, ladies and gentlemen. I'm
so thrilled to be here in this beautiful place."

RAQUEL WELCH: "The things I could do if I wasn't sponsored by Coca Cola."

SOPHIA LOREN: "This is mine and no one can touch it."

MIA FARROW: "Marriage without promises—it'd be so groovy."

ALI MacGRAW: "I can get high on my fantasies."

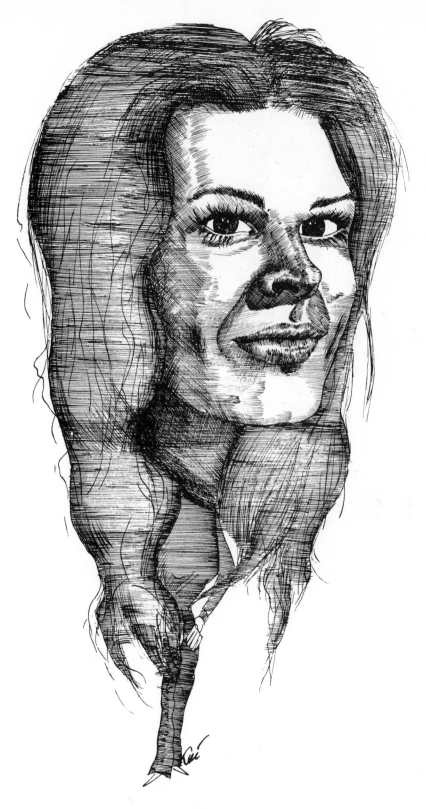

CANDICE BERGEN: "I'm great at the physical stuff—running, riding, jumping. Acting—that's another story."

PAUL NEWMAN: "Don't call us, we'll call you."

ROBERT REDFORD: "The flawed hero is the movie I'm
living myself."

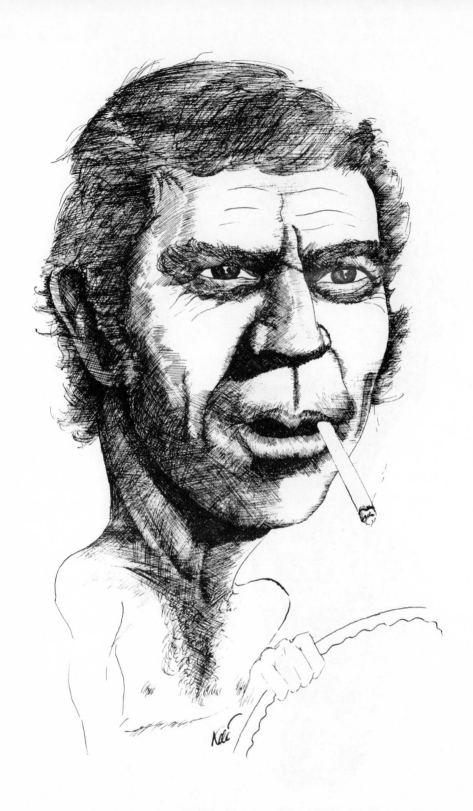

STEVE McQUEEN: "I've always had itchy feet . . ."

JACK NICHOLSON: "I've balled everybody, taken drugs, and gone somewhere."

DENNIS HOPPER :"Uh, we gotta save the movie industry, man." (Plane full of drug addicts.) "He's a pilgrim, he'a a preacher, and a problem when he's stoned."

PETER FONDA: "Part of my gig as an actor is to be able to speak out." "I have to tell it like it is, man."

JANE FONDA: "They're only organic Vitamins my father
gave me."

TONY CURTIS: "I quit, cigarettes, that is. Tobacco, that is." "Oh the perils of the weed."

SHIRLEY MacLAINE: "Don't fall Off the Mountain."

DUSTIN HOFFMAN: "There is something about making love
that changes things dramatically."

ELLIOTT GOULD: "I'm scared as hell about driving Bibi
Andersson . . . I get rigid with fright. I want to jump out
and hail a taxicab."

MARLON BRANDO: "People create me. So who I am is of
no importance."

GEORGE C. SCOTT: "The audience is a dark thing, a peculiar
animal, an enemy that must be assaulted and won."

LAUREN BACALL: "Wow."

CAROL CHANNING: "The funniest female to hit the boards since Fannie Brice and Beatrice Lillie."—John Chapman.

KATHERINE HEPBURN: "Coco expressed no opinion about my clothes, she just looked at me and probably hoped I could act."

JOHN WAYNE: "I don't act, I react."

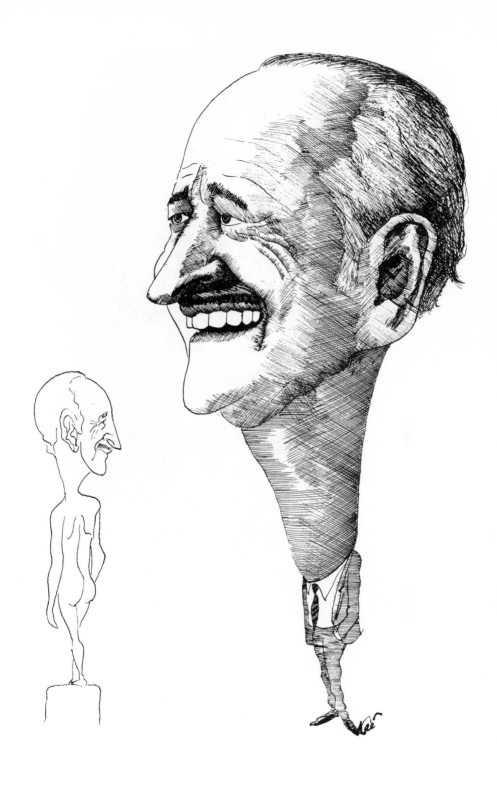

DAVID NIVEN: "Anglo-Saxon type 2008."

LIZ TAYLOR: "If you stay up late, Richard, it'll cost you
another present."

MAE WEST: "I think I've got the new touch—I've always been ahead of my time."

ROBERT BLACKWELL: Women

ZSA ZSA GABOR: "I suppose I'm the biggest ham in the business, darling."

RED SKELTON: "If a guy loses everything he has, he doesn't have to go out in the desert and shoot himself. All he's got to do is go to his room, turn on the airconditioning and freeze to death."

DANNY KAYE: "The show must go on . . ."

LUCILLE BALL: "Repeat after me: I love Lucy, I loved Lucy, and I will love Lucy."

GRAHAM KERR: "The gourmet galloping across five
continents."

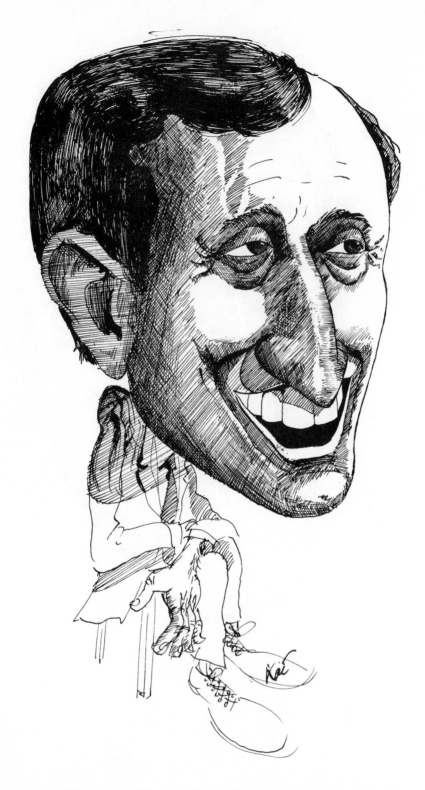

DAVID FROST: "I adore all women—because they dance
backwards."

JOHNNY CARSON: "There's always been something running against me . . . But you don't compete against the competition, but against yourself."

DICK CAVETT: "I'm funnier than Chet Huntley, taller than Mickey Rooney, and as pure and honest as Newark, New Jersey."

MERV GRIFFIN: "We're all going to have fun lying about guests—I wanted to announce Howard Hughes and Charles Lindbergh, but CBS said that 'It'd be too much.'"

DAVID SUSSKIND: "Full-time yakker."

WALTER CRONKITE: "Utterly unflappable."

JIM BOUTON: (As newscaster.) " . . . and in college basketball
tonight, it's the Mets vs Phillies."

DENNY McLAIN: "Yes I'm stupid and greedy."

JOE NAMATH: "Sure I cussed the cop out, and I was wrong
to do it . . . But I was sober."

WILT CHAMBERLAIN: "They'll know my name again."

BOBBIE ORR: "He's so good that he can spoil the game for everybody." — Trainer.

DEREK SANDERSON: "Big Bad Bruin."

LEE TREVINO: "You might go into those discotheques at 24, but if you stay long enough, you'll come out forty-seven." (At Copa del Mundo.)

TONY JACKLIN: "I'm concentrating on becoming the greatest player in the world."

ROD LAVER: "Tennis, like love, is a ladies' game."

ARTHUR ASHE: "Men don't want to give up money just for girls to play . . . why do we have to split our money with them?" "Rhythm & Blues are my best talents."

MRS. BILLIE JEAN KING: "Women's Lib . . . not so much
muscle and power, but a lot more tactics."

PELÉ (Edson Arantes do Nascimento): "A master techni-
cian."—Netto and Mello e Souza. Black Pearl (Pérola Negra) "I
could fight for my country or my friends, but not for one color."

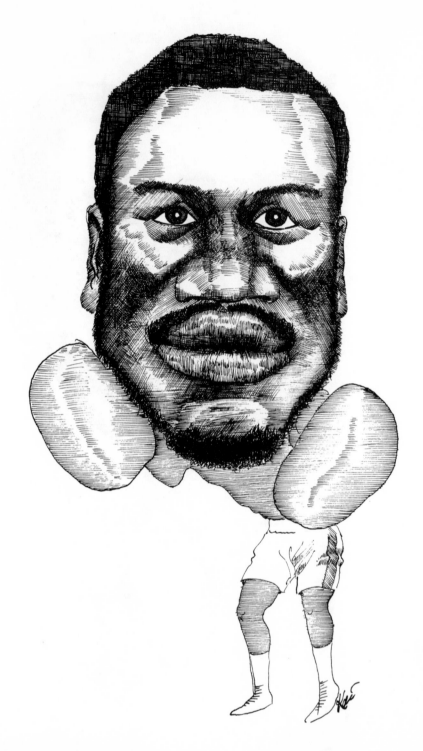

JOE FRAZIER: "If Clay gets a license to fight, we'll fight him,
until then we're willing to use him as a sparring partner—and
and we'll pay him."

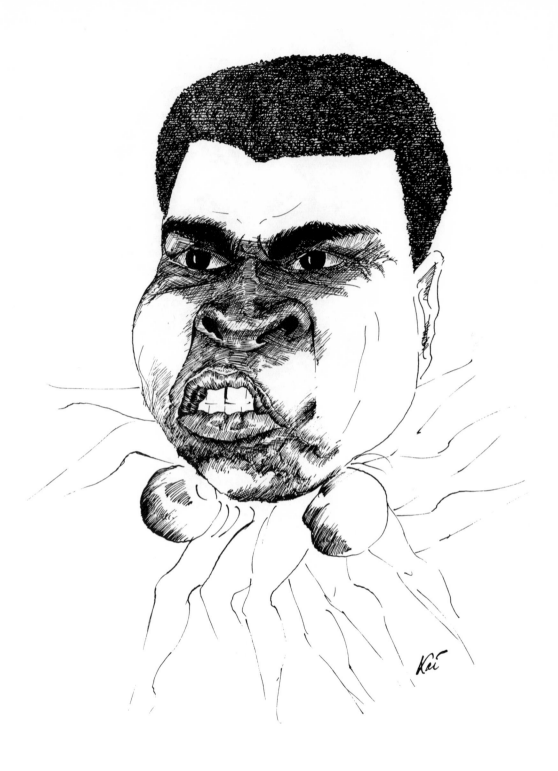

MUHAMMAD ALI: "No need to be sorry, if you call me by
my right name. I'm the Greatest, I really, really am."

CHARLES MANSON: "I may have been Jesus Christ, but I haven't decided yet what I am now."